I0478522

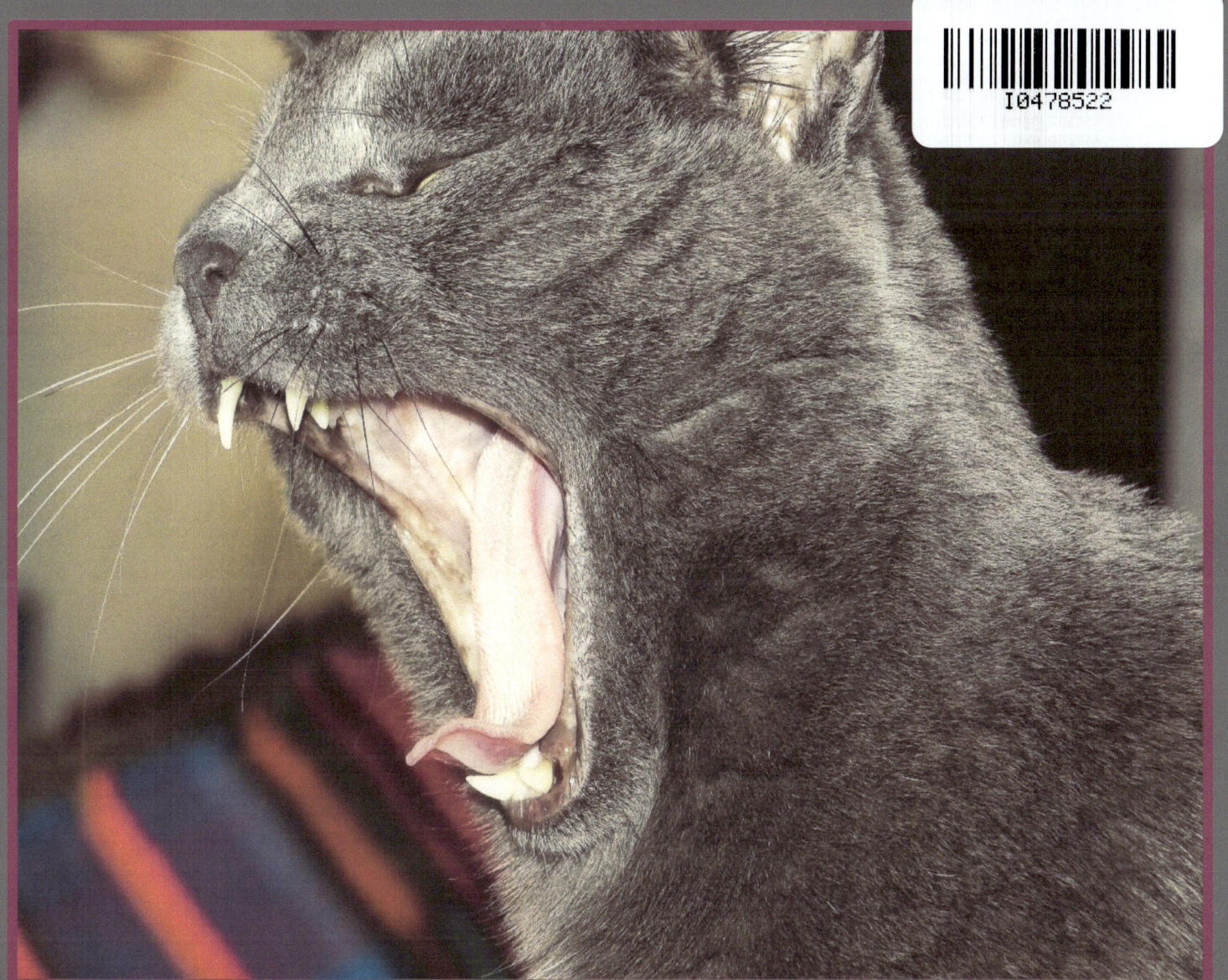

YURI YAWNS

IMAGES FROM ATWOOD

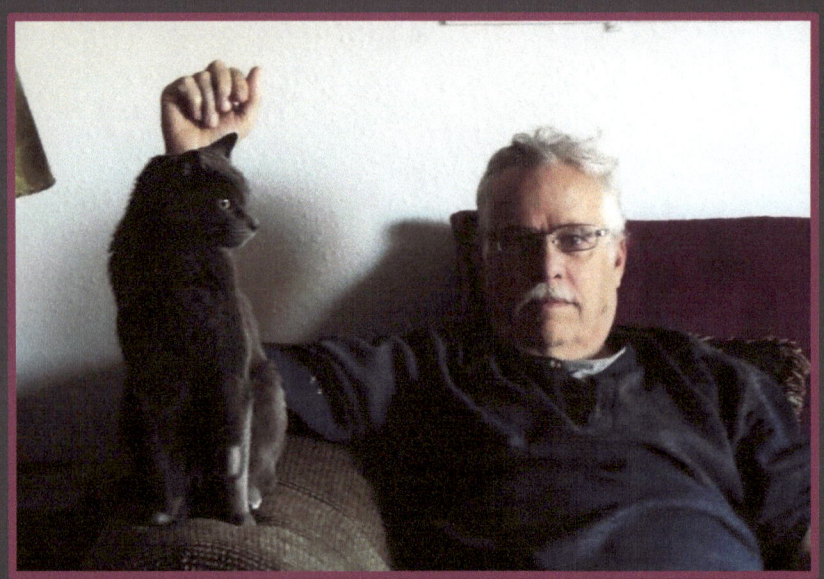

YURI YAWNS

IMAGES FROM ATWOOD

Copyright: 2016 by Echo Hill Arts Press, LLC.

All rights reserved, including the right to reproduce any part of this book.

ISBN: 13: 978-1541098091

ISBN: 10: 1541098099

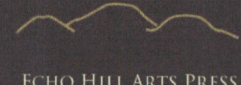

ECHO HILL ARTS PRESS

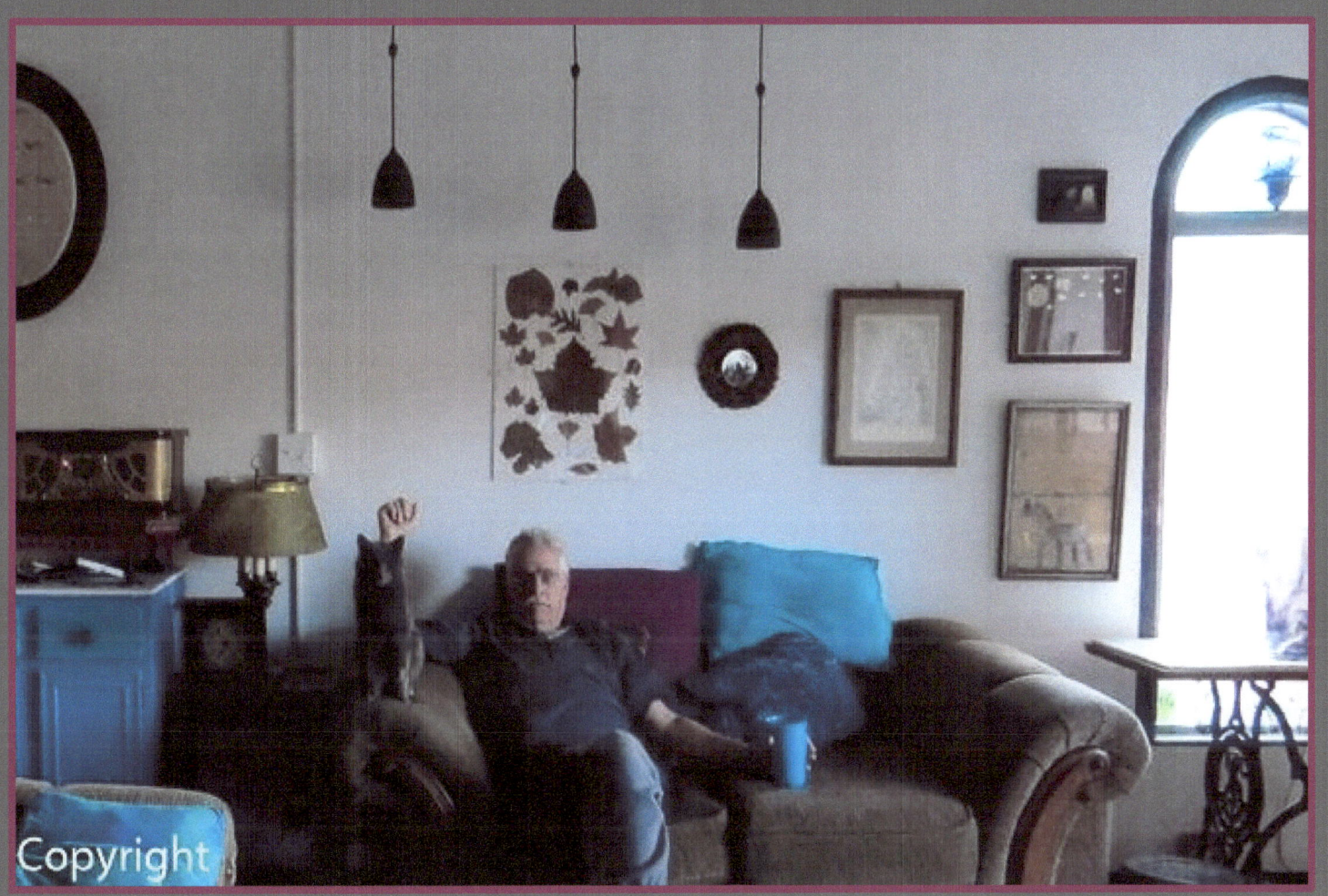

Copyright

This cool daddy has a brand-new cat.

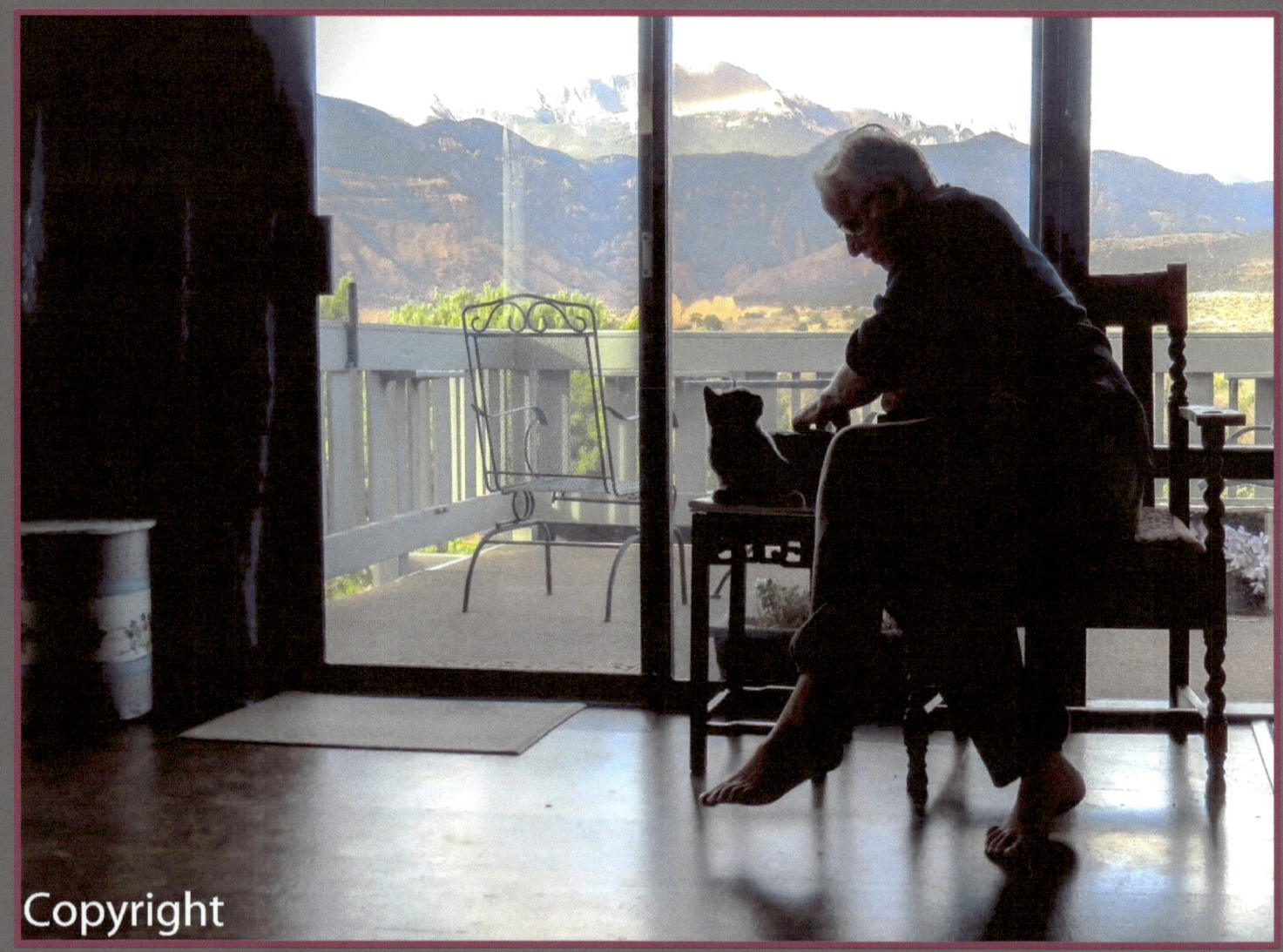

Copyright

He's named his new cat - Yuri.

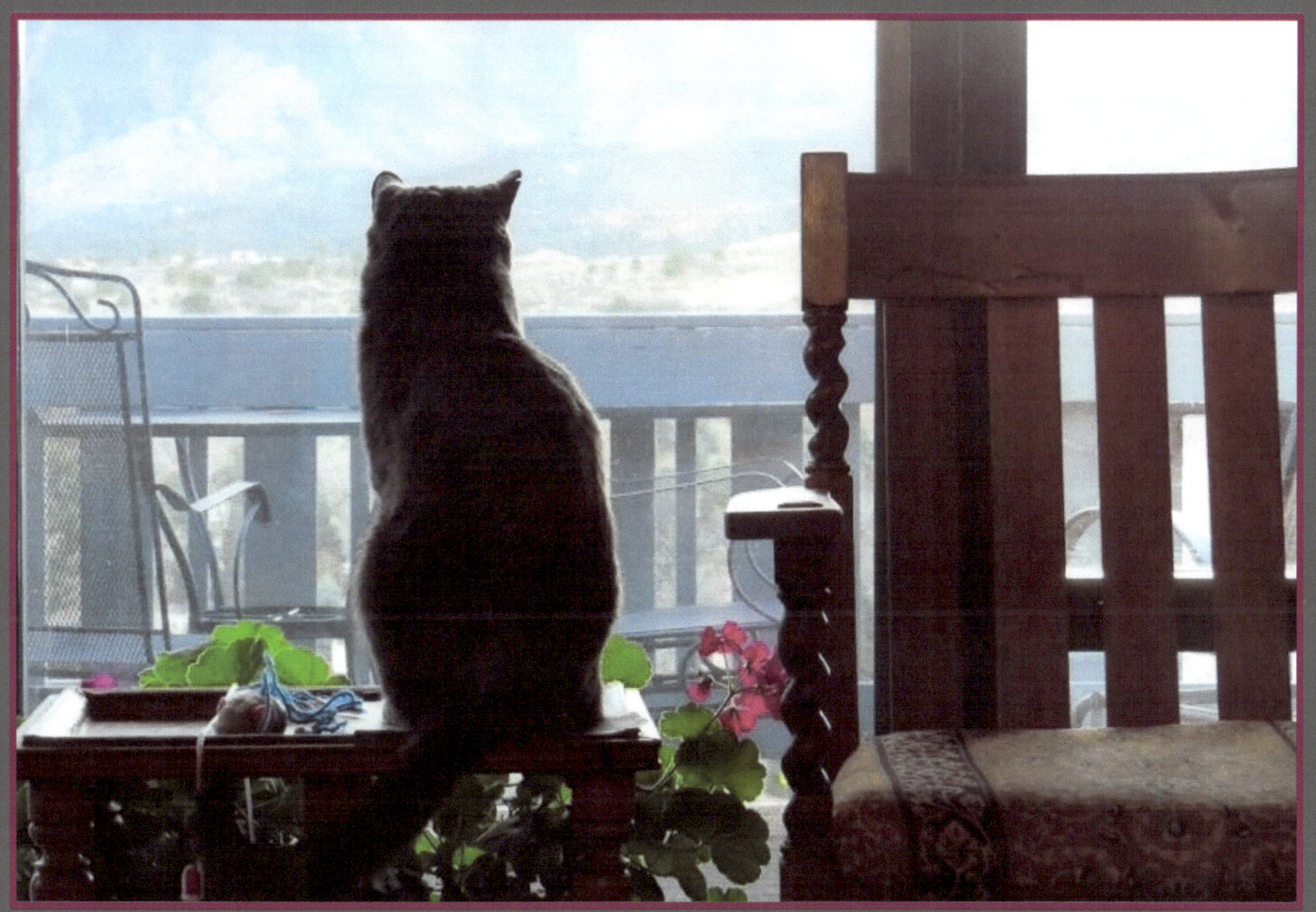

Yuri favors the private deck with hunting grounds beyond.

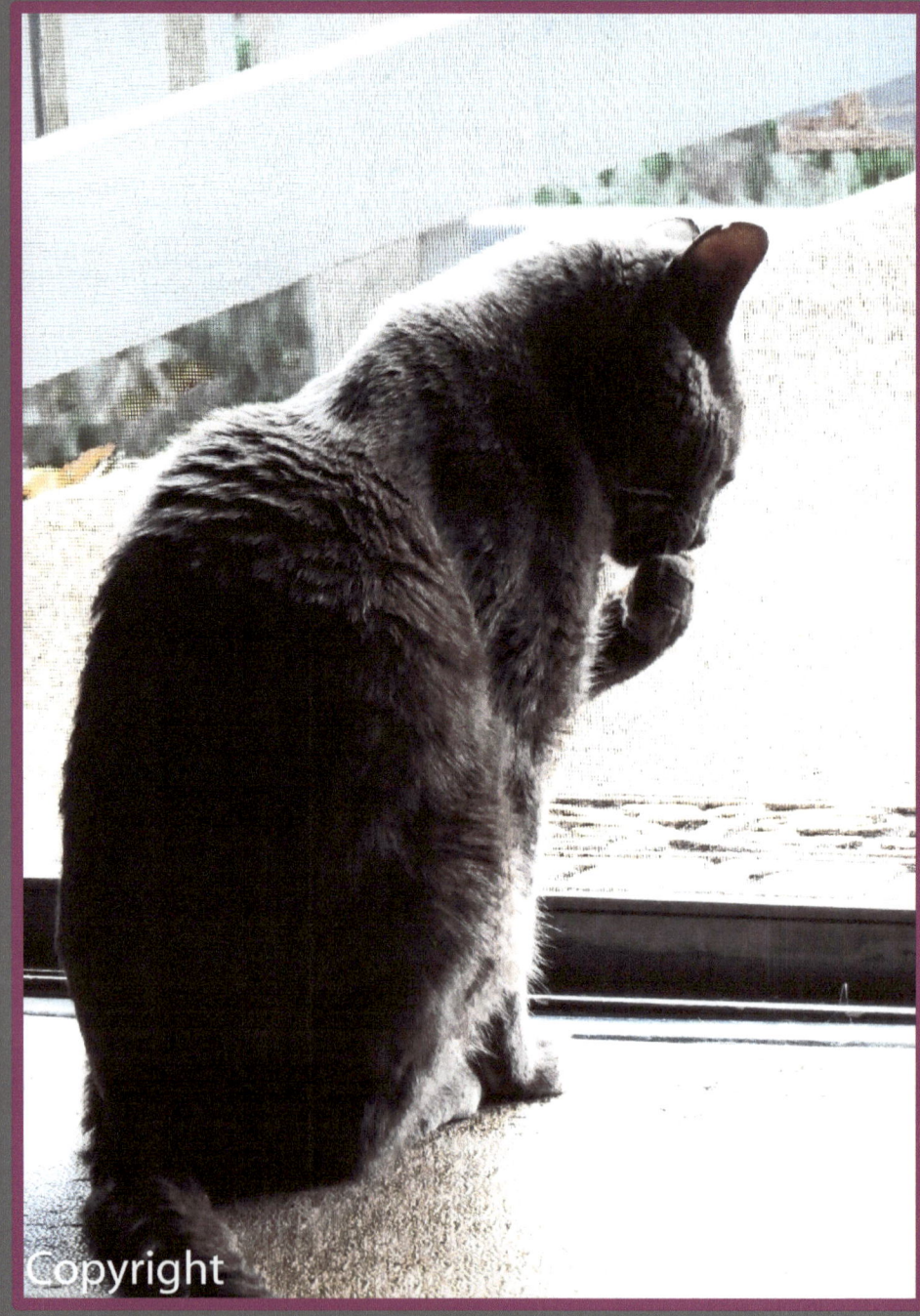

Copyright

After each hunt-catch-kill-eat session, he likes to freshen up.

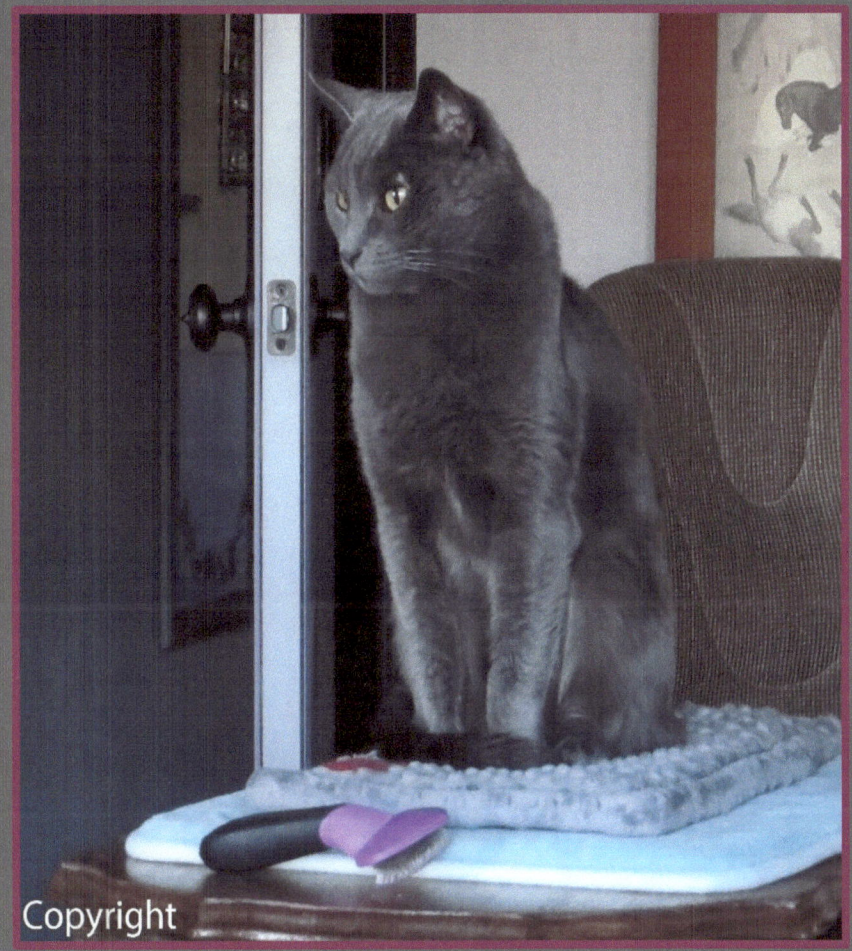

Copyright

Then, he likes to be combed.

He'll settle on his grooming table and wait patiently.

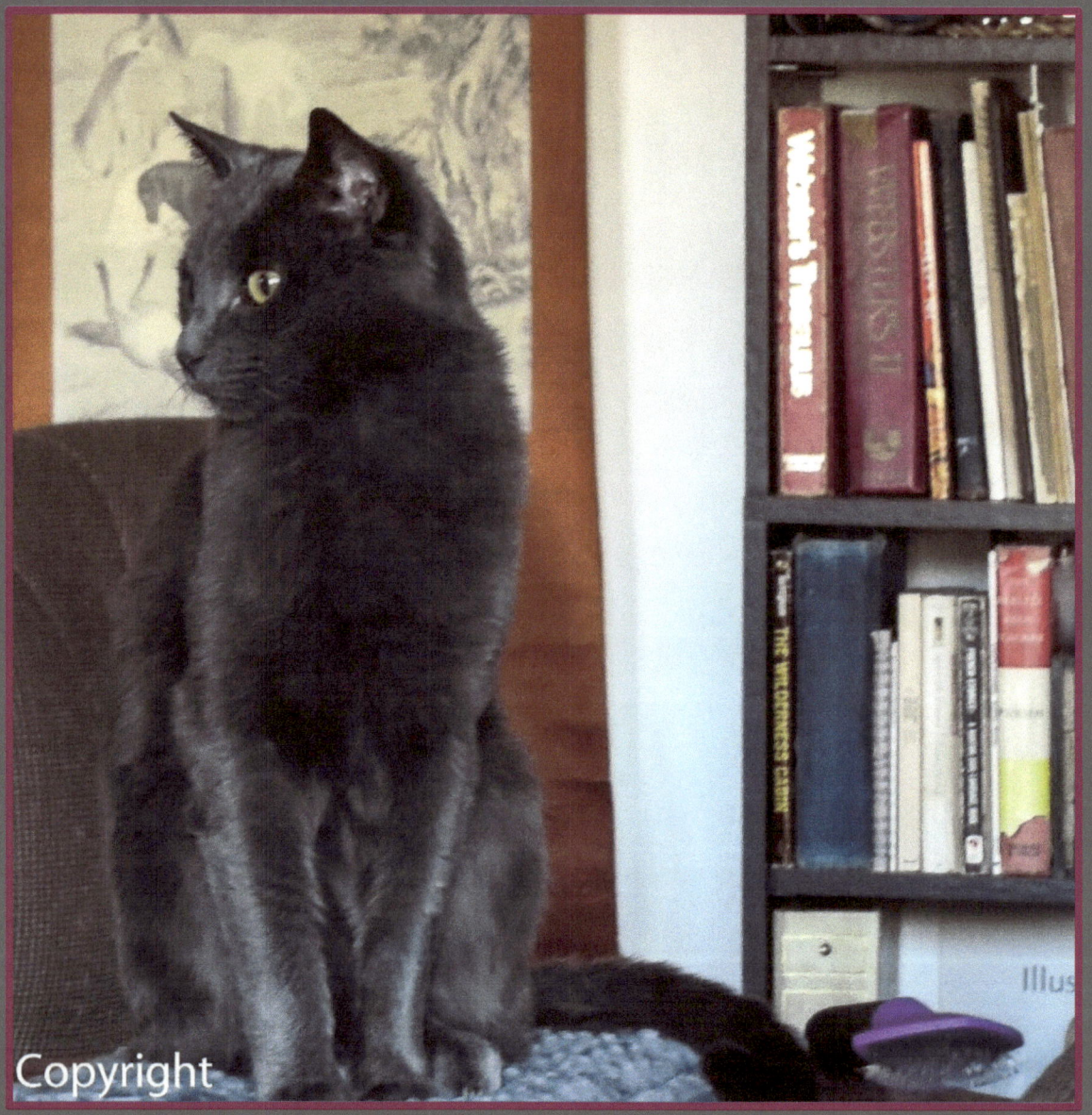

Copyright

It's not lost on this hunter that it's also a strategic lookout.

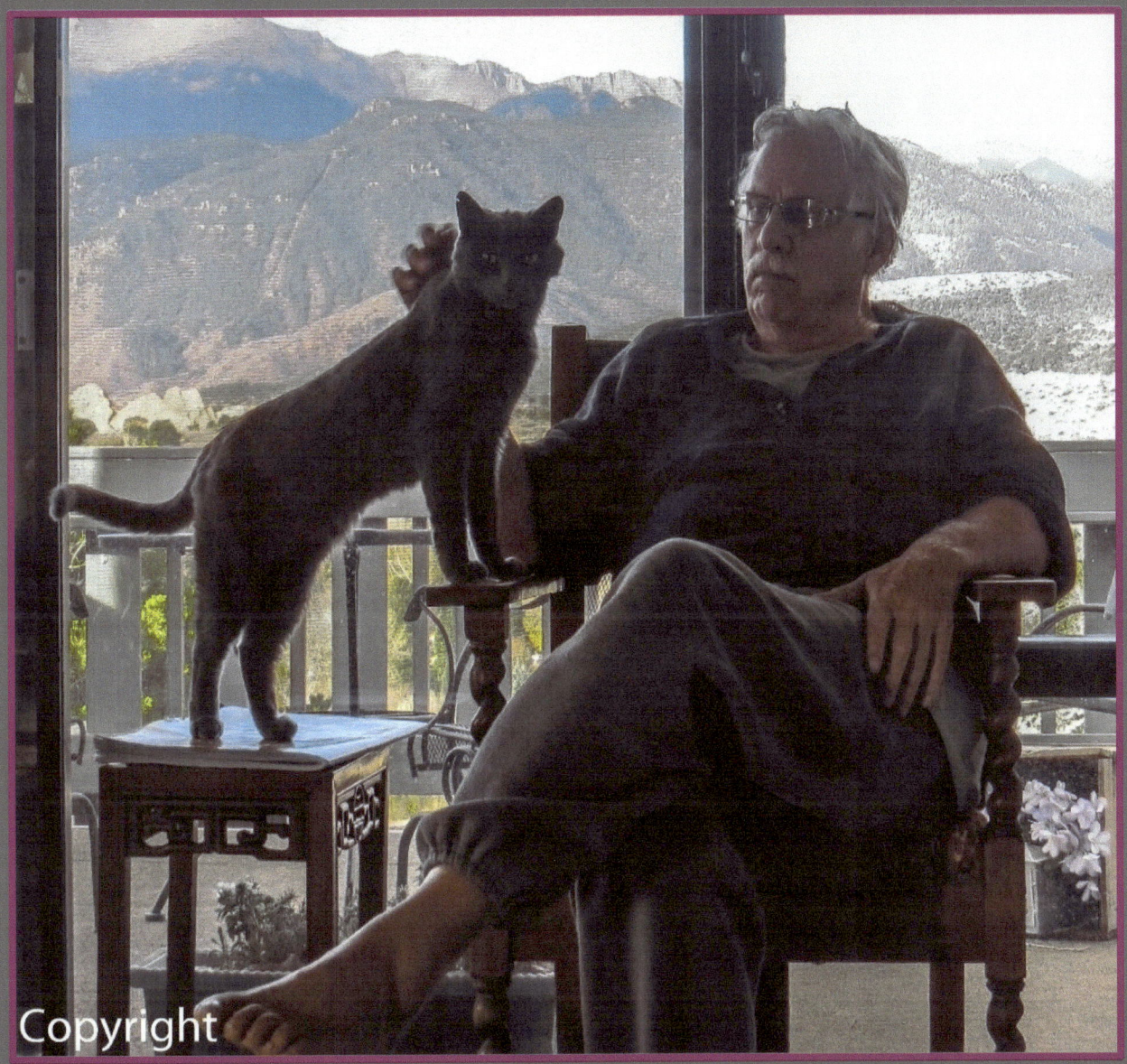

Copyright

"Hey, Yuri, what say we go get ourselves a Christmas tree?"

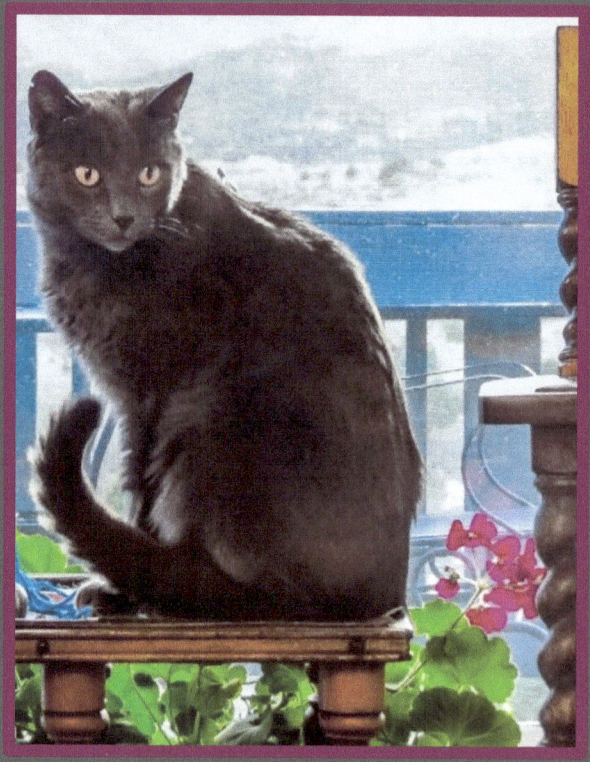

When it arrived, Yuri was transfixed.

"What the heck is that thing?" he meowed aloud.

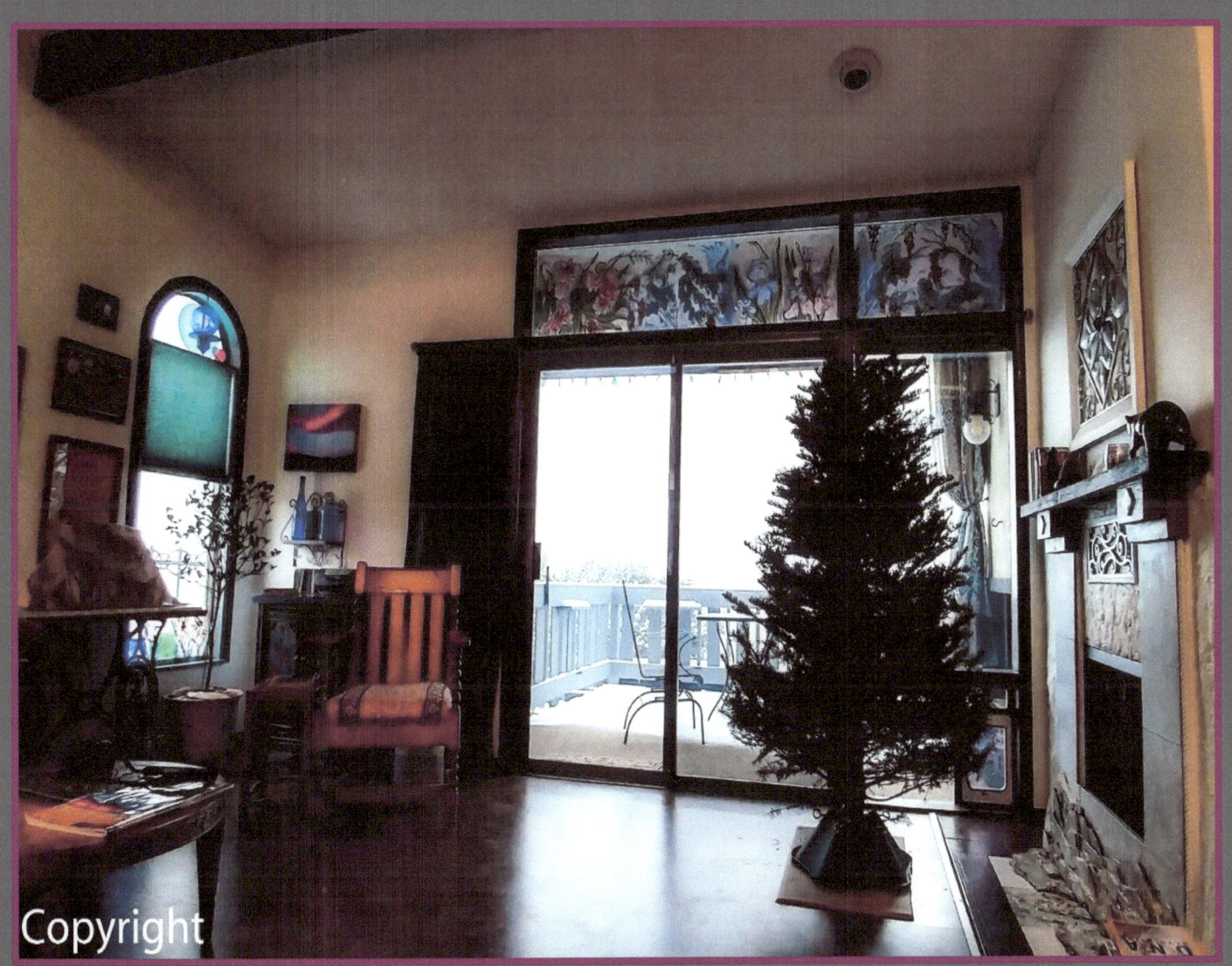

Copyright

"Just wait 'til she's dressed up," his dad assured him.

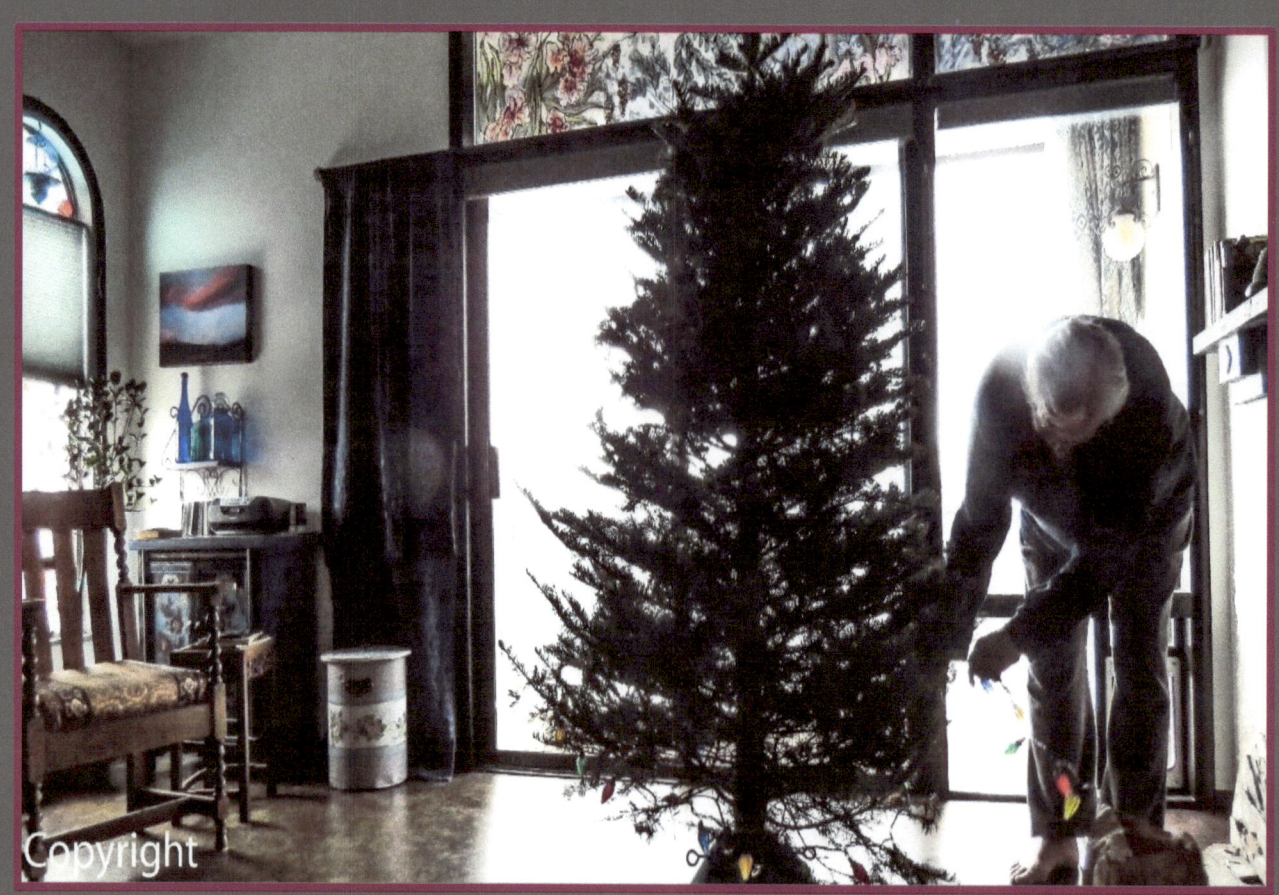

Copyright

Then he set to work decorating the house for the holidays.

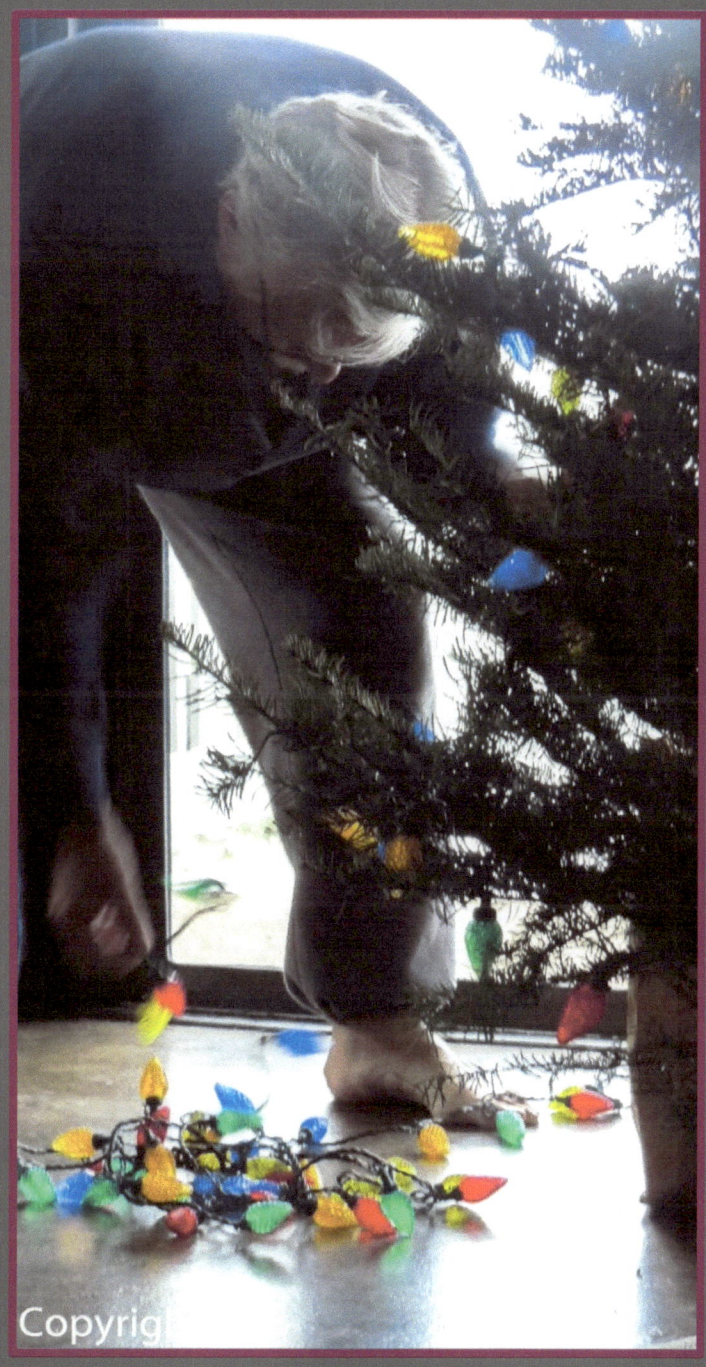

Copyrig

Finally, the big wad of lights had been strung

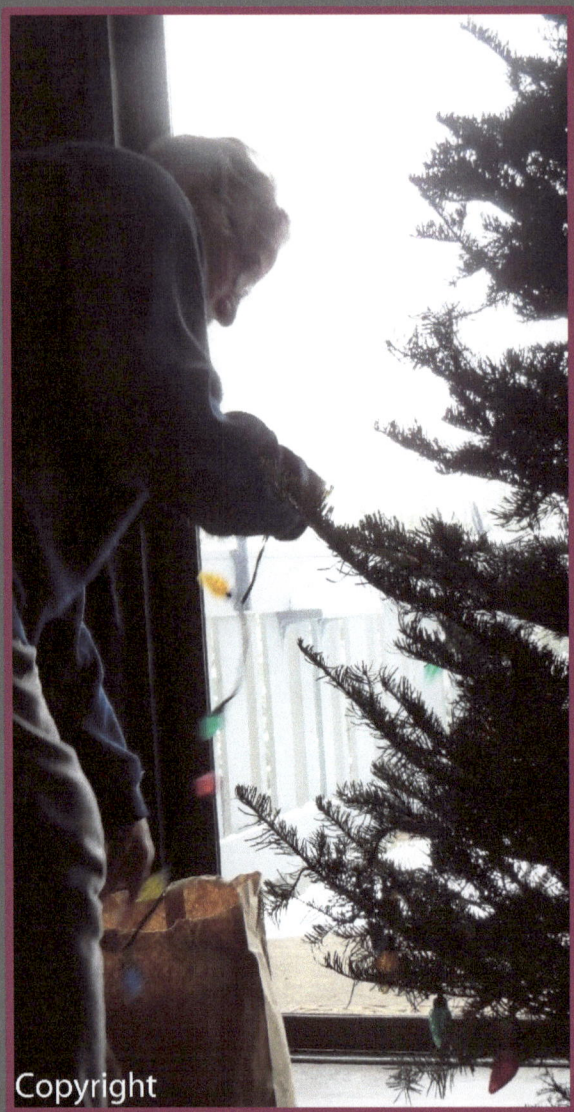
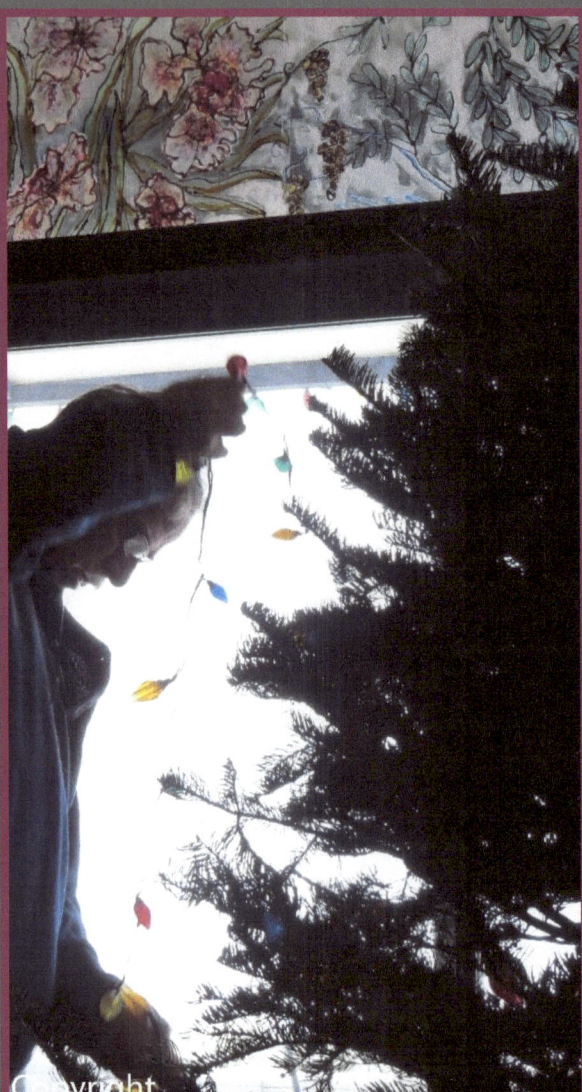

Copyright

Copyright

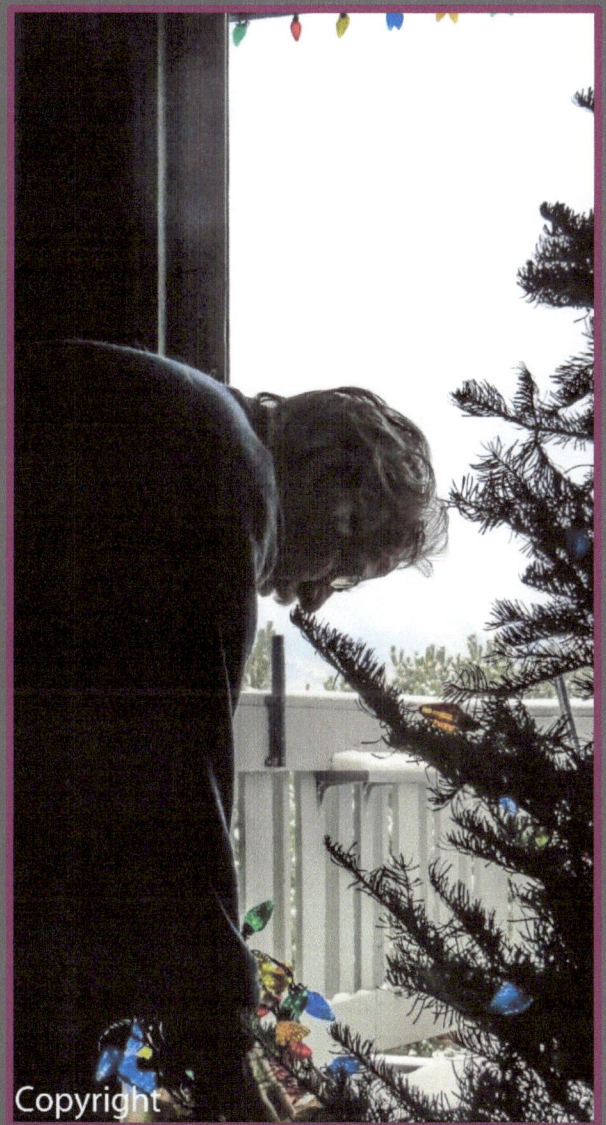
Copyright

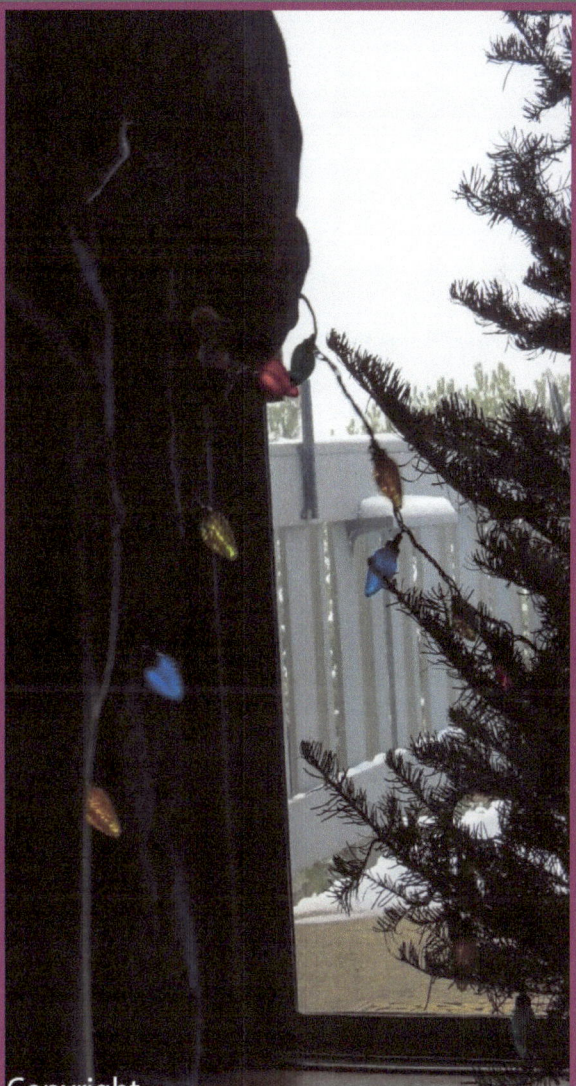
Copyright

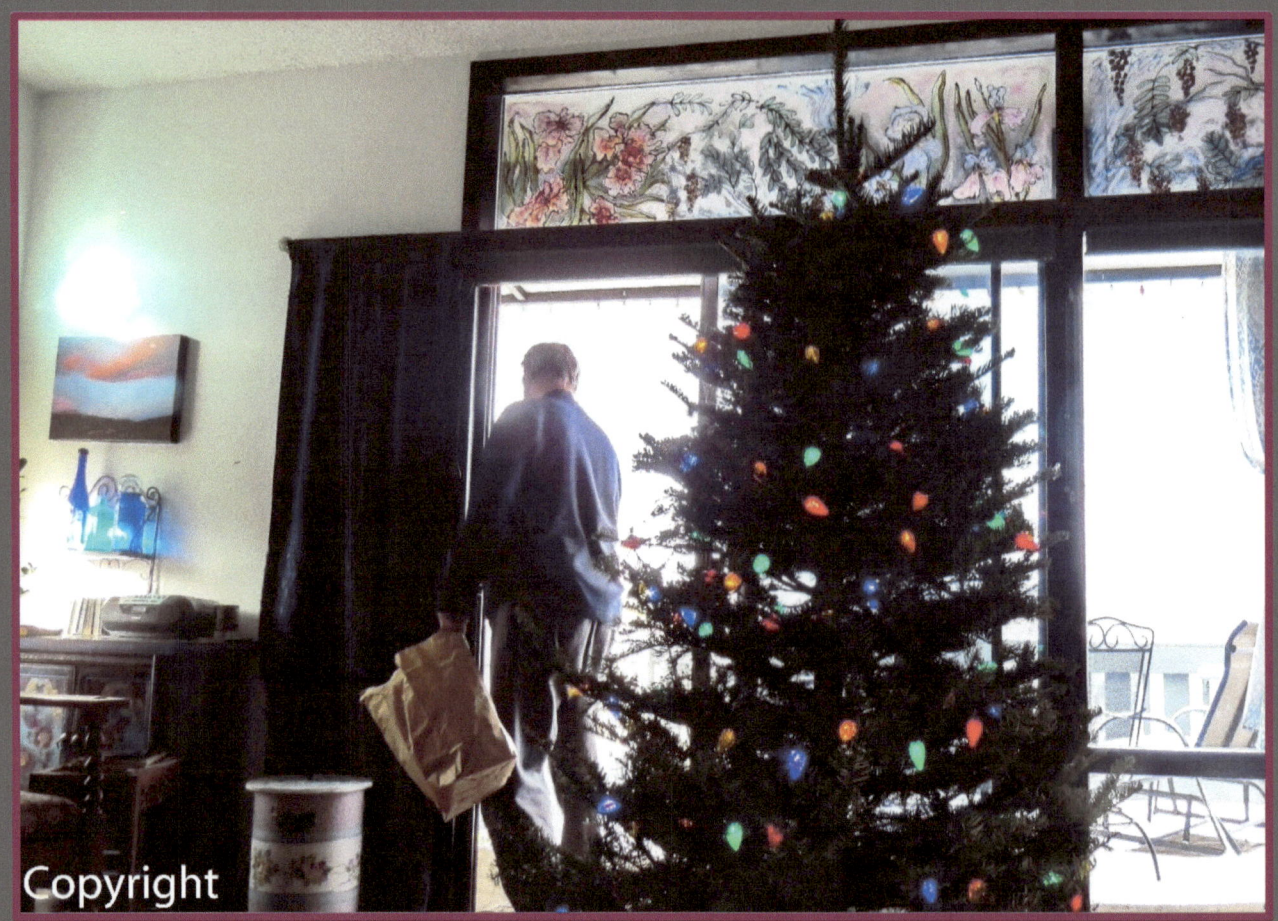
Copyright

And Cool Daddy's work for the day was all done.

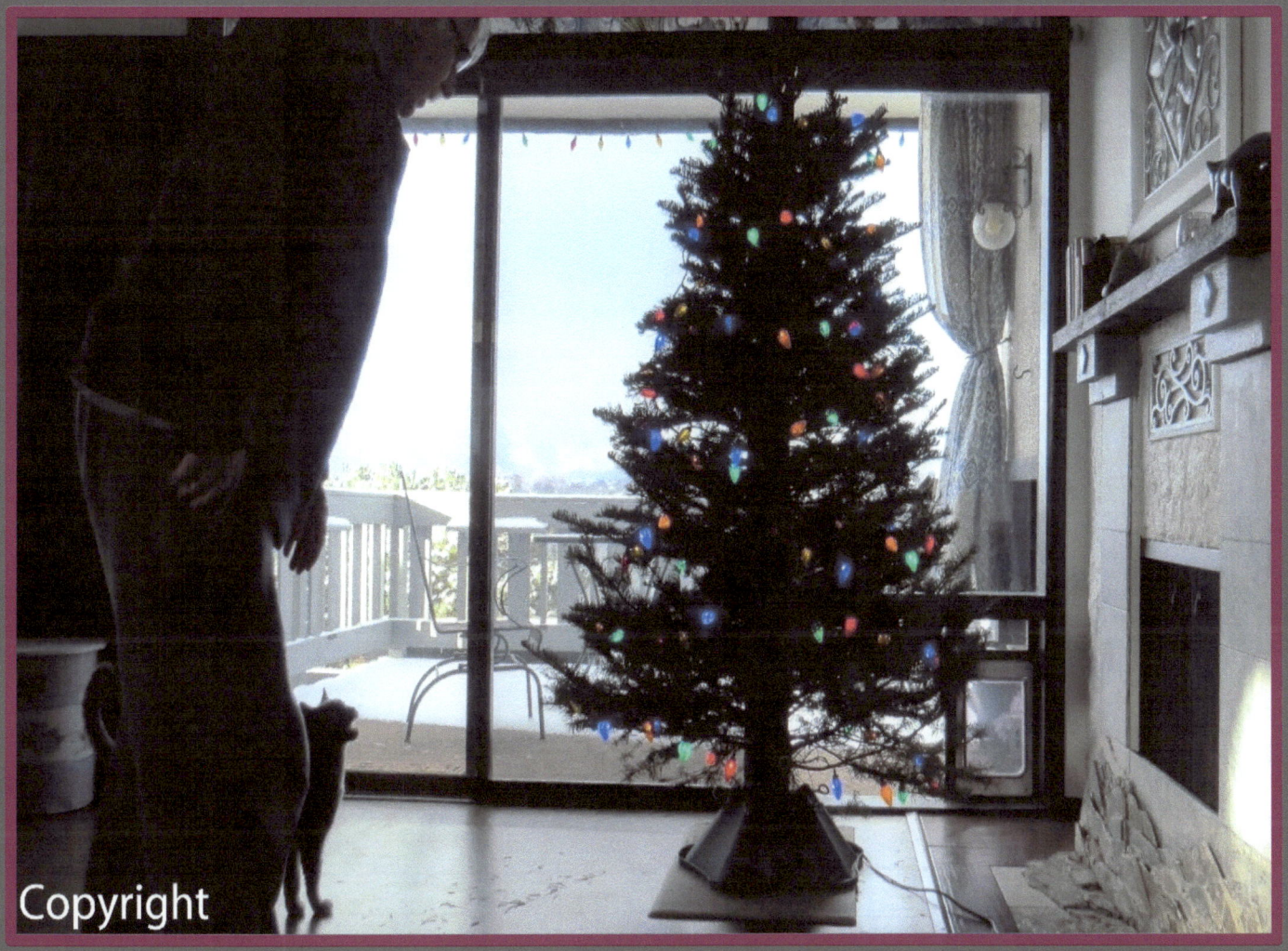
Copyright

Not one to keep his thoughts witheld, Yuri meowed quite loudly,

"WOW, Dad, I think it's very nice – which reminds me that I'm hungry."

As Yuri dined, the beauty of the season blazed glorious around him.

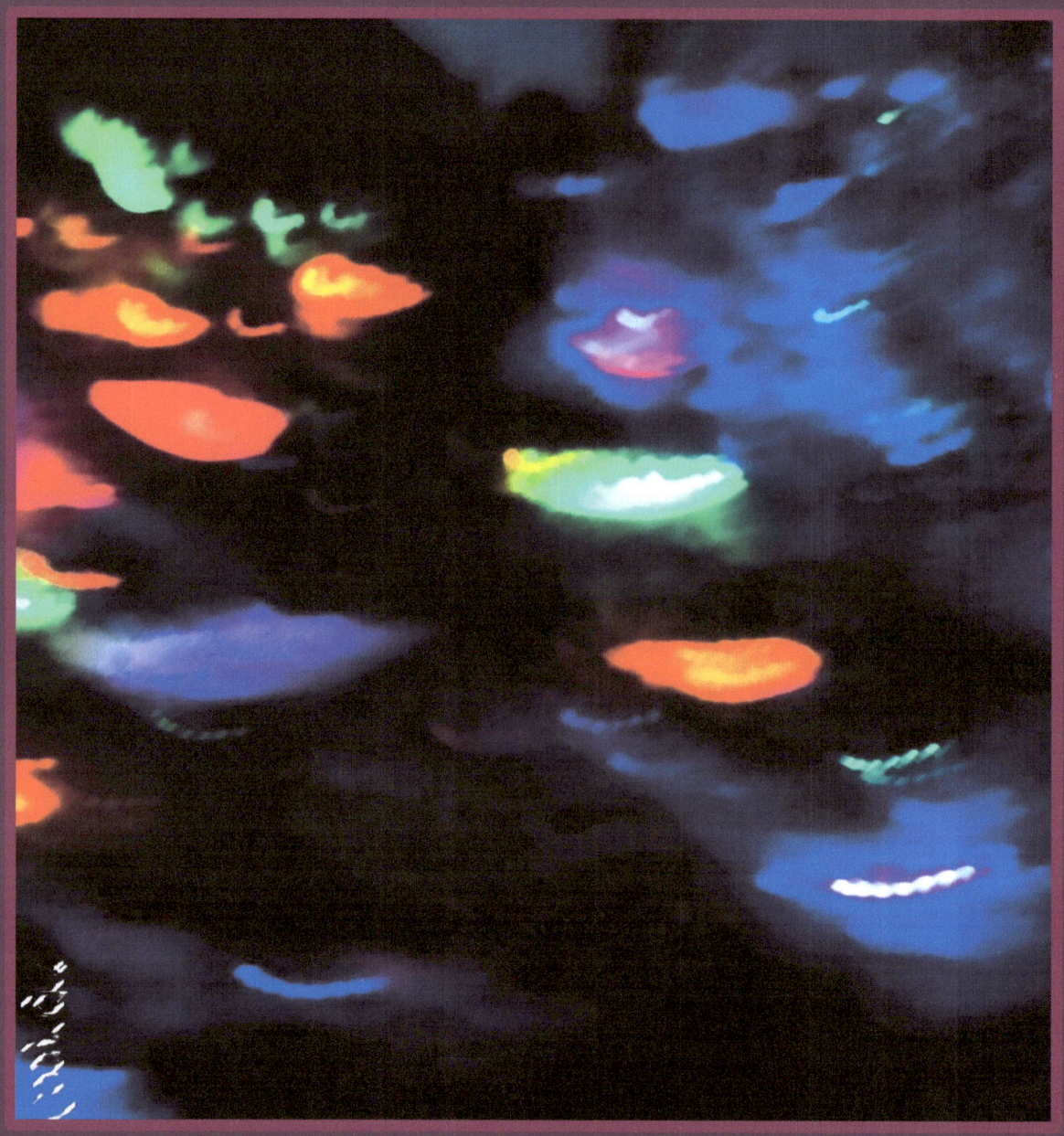

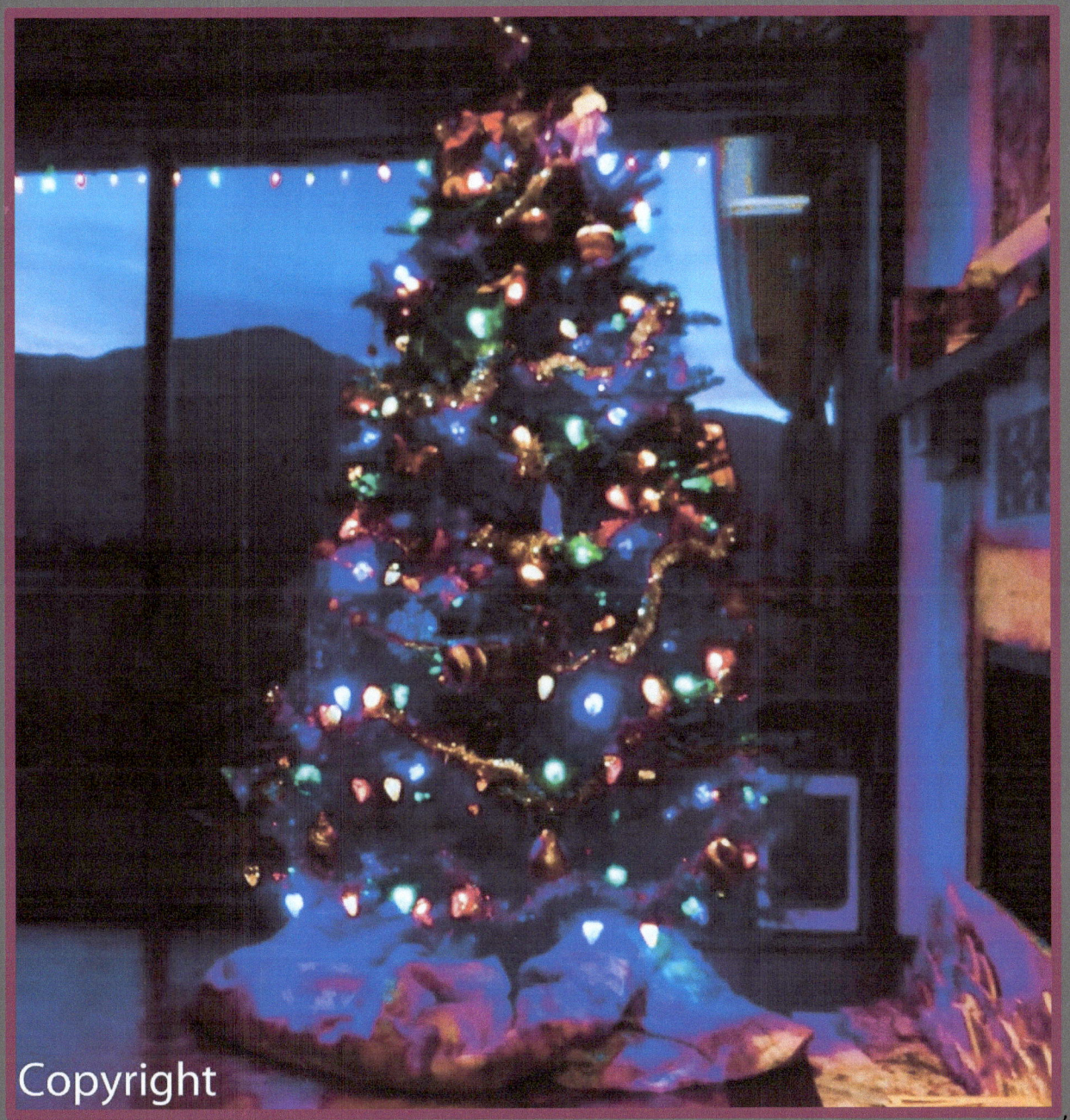

Copyright

How exciting!

In fact,

Overwhelmed by such a noble act,

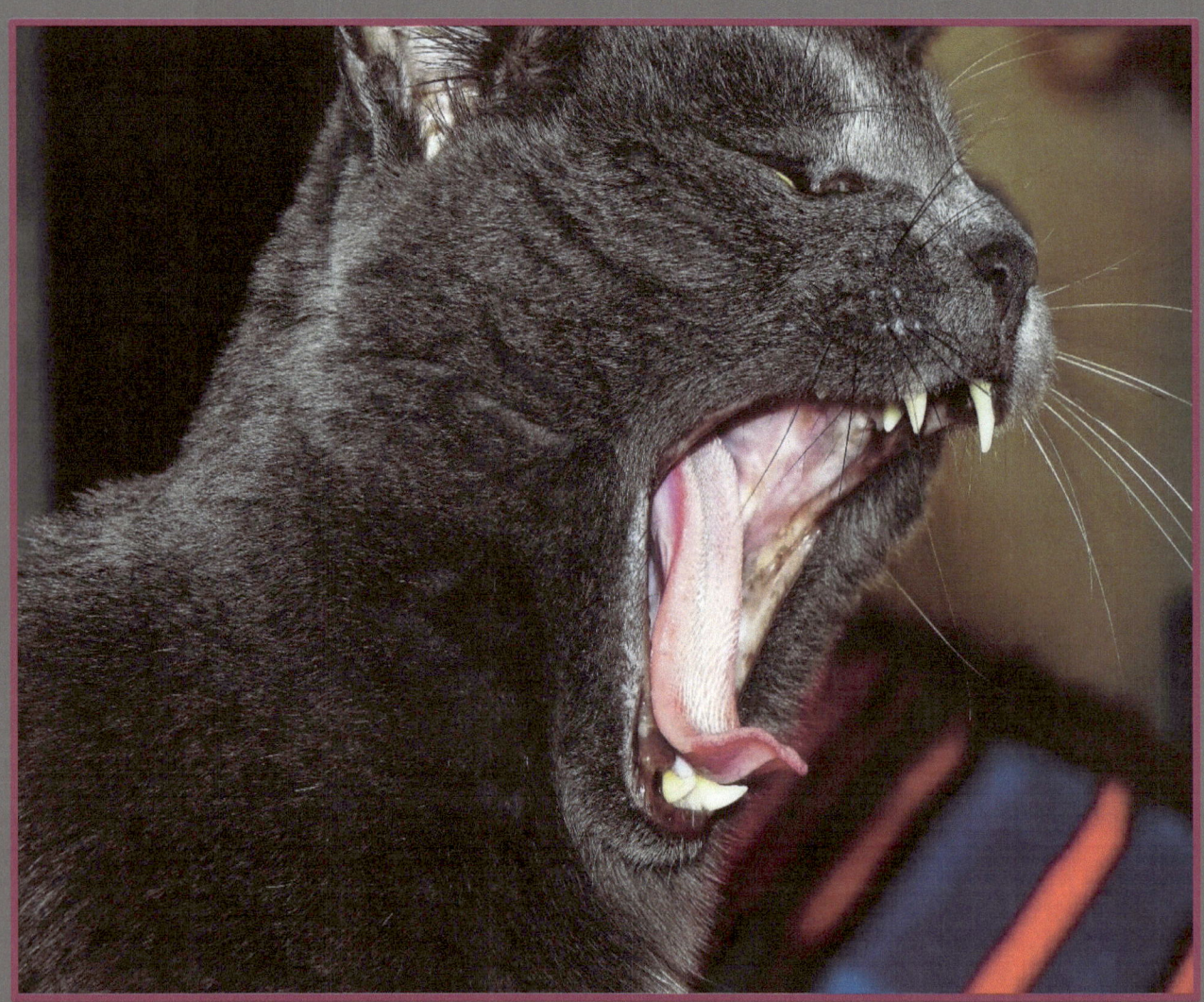

Yuri yawned wide,

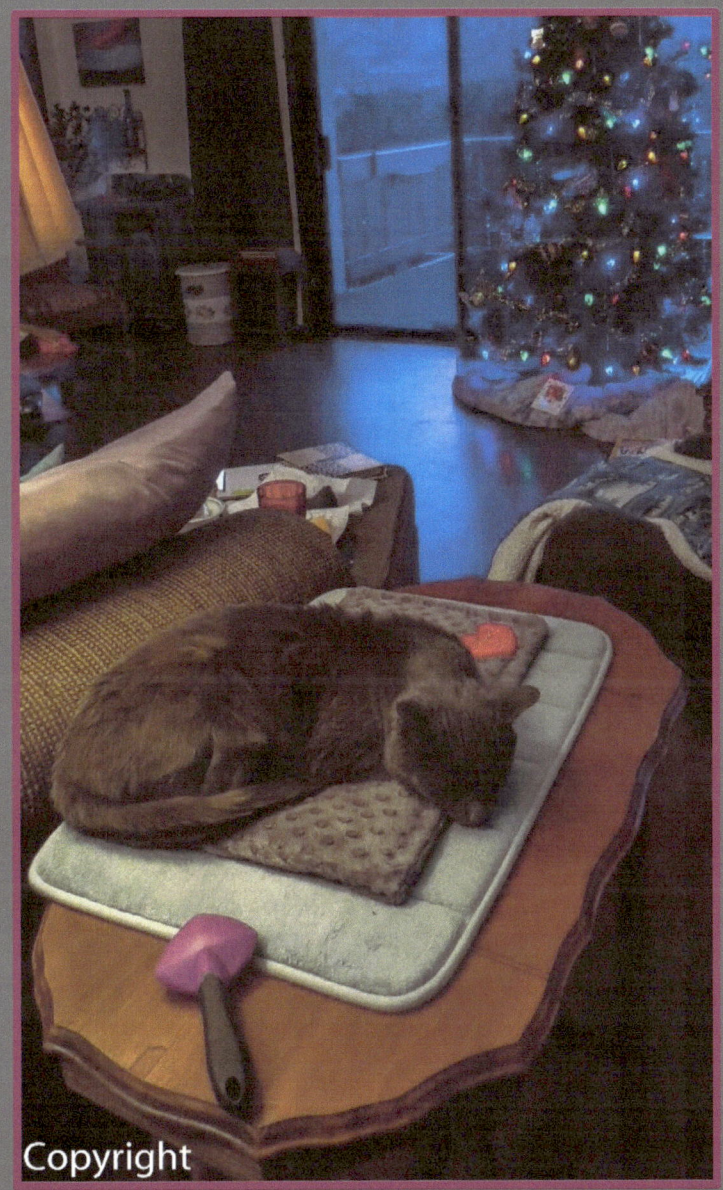
Copyright

And then took a nap.

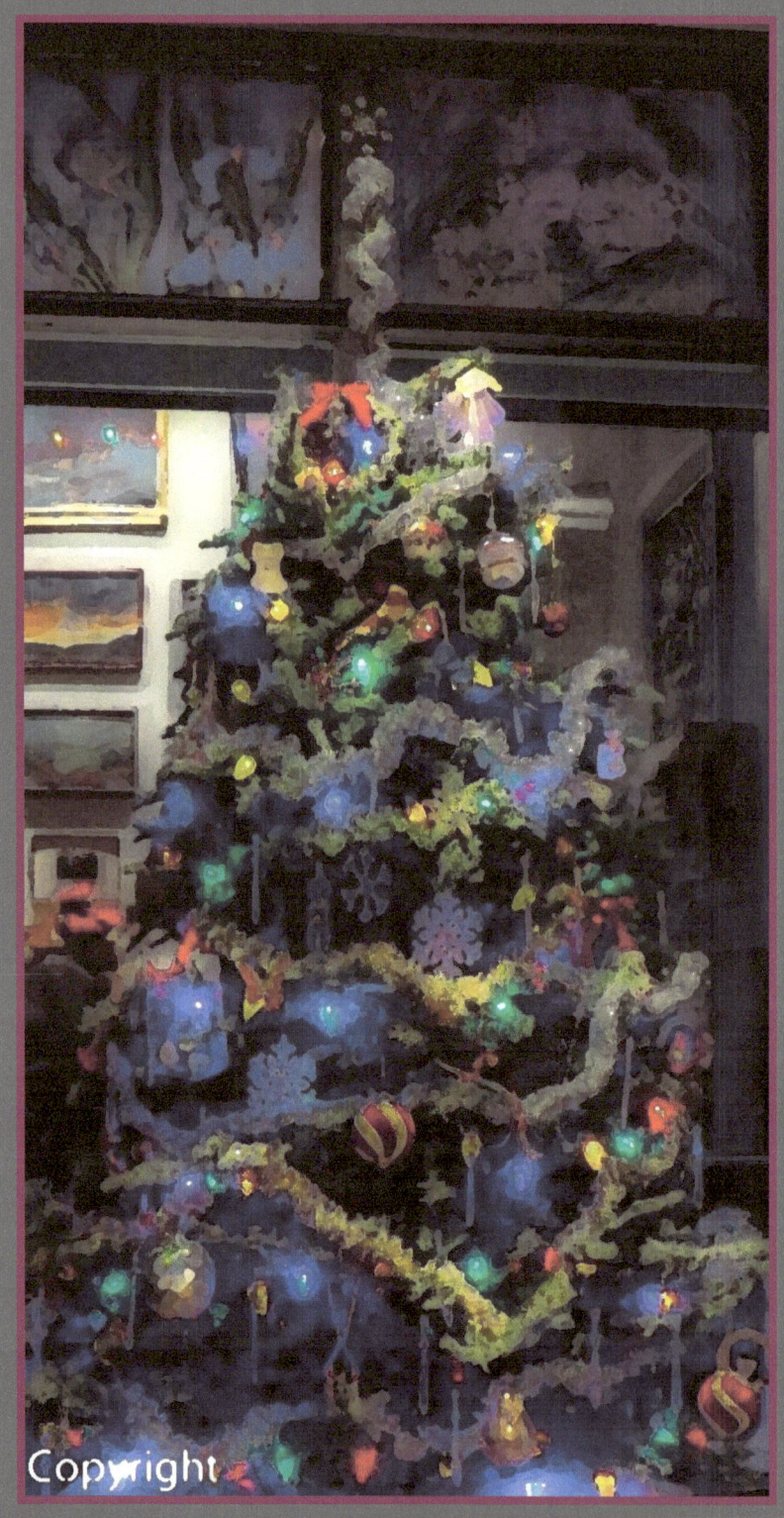
Copyright

Echo Hill Arts Press

is pleased to make a new line of

Images from Atwood

available through **Amazon.com.**

Diversionary Materials for
Areas of Waiting

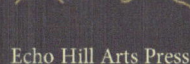

Echo Hill Arts Press

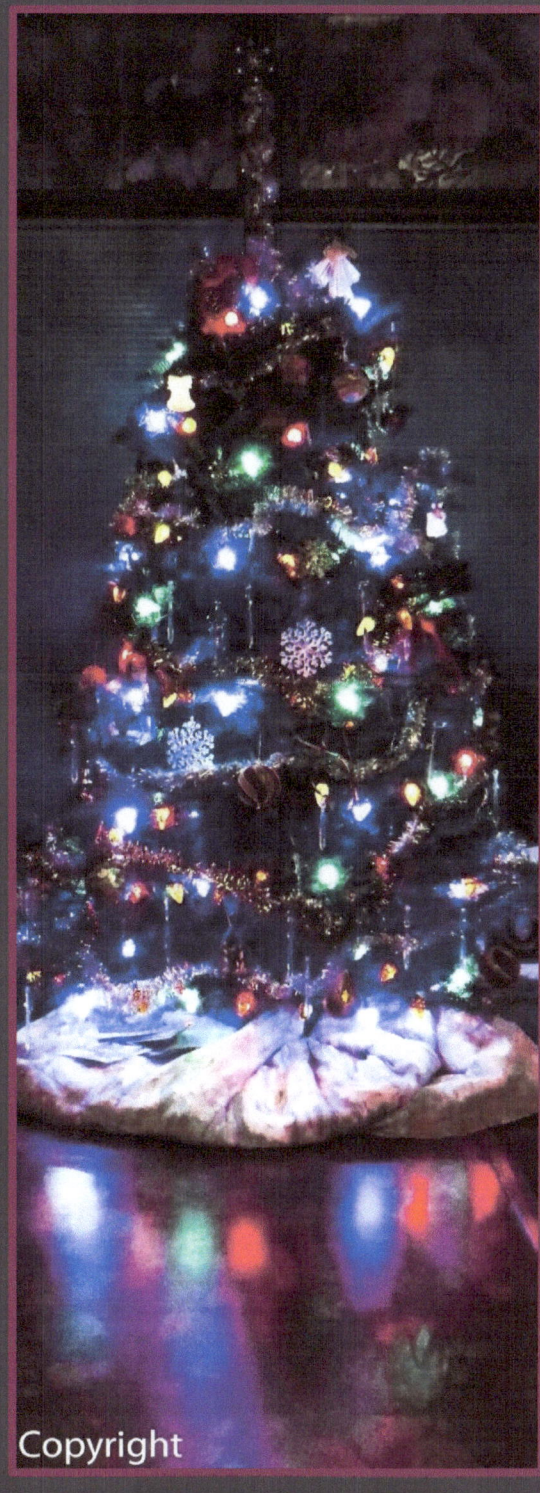

Copyright